AUTHENTICATED

UNLOCKING YOUR KINGDOM IDENTITY AND PROPHETIC PURPOSE

KOLANI T. SMITH

AUTHENTICATED
Unlocking Your Kingdom Identity and Prophetic Purpose

Kolani T. Smith
kolanislays@gmail.com

ISBN 978-1-949826-61-6
Printed in the USA.
All rights reserved

Published by: EAGLES GLOBAL PUBLISHING | Frisco, Texas
In conjunction with the 2023 Eagles Authors Course
Cover & interior designed by DestinedToPublish.com

DEDICATION

It has been such a humbling experience to have the opportunity from God to write this book, and to see the grace of support allotted to me in the process. For these reasons, I first thank and honor Abba Elohim for imparting into and commissioning me. Next, I want to thank my children, Denzel, Jonathan, and Naima, for unselfishly relinquishing their time with me to allow Mom to complete this project. I know the Lord will honor your sacrifice and bless you in ways I cannot fully communicate in words. You are my inheritance and greatest joy, God's gift to me and to the world. Please remember, I am so proud of you and the men and woman you are becoming each day. Always keep your heart open for God, and commit your gifts and lives to live out His purpose authentically and boldly. I love each of you uniquely but equally through eternity.

Mom

ACKNOWLEDGMENTS

I honor my parents, Sharion Frazier and Hubert Smith, Jr., for the positive ways each of them has shaped me into the woman of integrity I am. To my sister Tina, thank you for asking so many questions and causing me to dig deep to find answers. Bishop Ronald Logan, who treated me like a daughter and gave me wings to soar through adversity, I thank you. Apostle Dalyop "Daps" Gwom, thank you for sounding the shofar over my life that pulled the Asaph anointing from within me. Apostle Clyde and Prophetess Scheherazade Daniels, you two have loved me, encouraged me, and given me an open door and safe place to develop my Samuel anointing over the years. I publicly honor and thank you. Prophetess Sandee Hemphill, you are the OG of "Tough Love" and a true Apostolic Midwife. You taught me to be intentional, accurate, and prepared in season and out of season. A special thank you to my cousin, Pastor Randy T. Willis, Sr., and my Crimson Church International family, who have supported the School of the Warrior Bride Ministries from day one and allowed me to equip and minister in freedom as my authentic self. I honor you for your love, multitude of prayers, covering, encouragement, and affirmation. To my godmother Naomi "Muff" Crumb, thank you for your prayers, words of edification, and ever-watchful eye over my life. Pastors McClean, Denise, Luke, and Kelle Faw and the Joy Church family, thank you for always allowing me to be home. There is truly no place like Joy! I thank each one of my ministry partners for using the oil on your life to pour into me. I also thank each one of my mentees, who have accepted the call, pulled on the oil in my life, and helped refine me as a mentor. Finally, to my international counsel of Apostles, Bishops, and Prophets, and EITI community, who encouraged me to jump in the River and go beyond waist deep, thank you for both the pull and the push. I love you all and pray God blesses you as only He can.

Prophetess Kolani

God is revealing your story and rewriting your narrative.

FOREWORD

Grace and Peace,

Prophetess Kolani has been a strong prophetic voice, equipper, and influencer for many years. She has served as a handmaiden, coach, and mentor to many emerging prophets, and an advisor to established prophets as well as apostles. I met her in 2011, when she was teaching for The Eagles Network (TEN) Worldwide. She has been a mentor and leadership advisor for me ever since. Prophetess Kolani was one of my first prophetic mentors, who unlocked my prophetic destiny by spending time with me and encouraging me to speak up. Over the years, Prophetess Kolani has equipped and helped to birth many prophetic teams by helping each individual to discover their Kingdom identity within their gifts.

Authenticated: Unlocking Your Kingdom Identity and Prophetic Purpose will be a great resource in addition to her hands-on approach to teaching and building the Kingdom of God. Readers will walk away knowing who they are in God and feeling empowered to serve out their God-given identity.

Katrina R. Carter

APOSTLE
HEAVENLY DOVE MINISTRIES
WWW.HEAVENLYDOVEMINISTRIES.ORG

DIRECTOR OF THE EAGLES NETWORK (TEN) WORLDWIDE
WWW.TENWORLDWIDE.ORG

ENDORSEMENTS

If there was ever a time to get more excited about your identity in the Kingdom, it is now! Through facilitating the Kingdom Identity class, Prophetess Kolani has emphasized the richness of knowing who we are in the Kingdom. Her warm and encouraging spirit allows the peace of God to flow through her as she invites others to learn and understand their true identity in Christ.

Sesha Woodard

AUTHOR
DROPPING SEEDS IN MOTION, OWNER AND FOUNDER
WWW.DROPPINGSEEDSINMOTION.COM

Greetings in the Name of Our Lord and Savior Jesus Christ. My name is Pastor Randy T. Willis, Sr., and I am the Senior Pastor of Crimson Church International located in Boston, Massachusetts. I am honored to speak about the personality of Prophetess Kolani Smith. This powerful woman of God is a great asset to the ministry. She preaches the Word with power and diction. Spiritually speaking, when she preaches the Word, it is like a two-edged sword twirling in both directions. She rightly divides the word of truth with encouragement, correction, healing, and deliverance. I am proud to say that she is a part of our ministry. Prophetess Kolani is faithful and dependable. She is an awesome woman of God, and I am honored to be her spiritual mentor, pastor, and cousin.

Pastor Randy T. Willis, Sr.
CRIMSON CHURCH INTERNATIONAL

I am a witness of the amazing spirit that is Prophet Kolani Smith. She is a greatly anointed and gifted teacher, seamstress, dancer, shifter, and midwife to the birthing of many Prophets of God. When she flows, whether in dance or speaking, the Spirit of God invades your atmosphere so that you can see and hear Him with clarity. This woman is multitalented as well, teaching and exhorting people to tap into their creative vein with painting, acting, and theatrical production. There is no limit to how far she can take you, because of how far she is willing to go in God. I have no doubt this literary work of art will enhance in every way as it is taken in!

THANKS AND REGARDS,

Prophet and Psalmist Doneta Dawson
KINGDOM ARTS FUZION AND DONETA DAWSON MINISTRIES

Kingdom identity supersedes denomination, church affiliation, class, gender, and race. Kingdom identity is a declaration that God is the authority, especially for those of us who believe. We are citizens of God's territory. Few people understand this existence; Prophetess Kolani is one of them. This woman of God has used her prophetic gift to bless the Kingdom across genres. I've witnessed firsthand her gift of prophetic ministry to open people's hearts to God's Holy Spirit, people who otherwise never would have been open to such an experience. I highly recommend any illumination offered by Prophetess Kolani regarding Kingdom identity. God has given her a unique and balanced perspective concerning the Kingdom. I believe God will speak to your heart through this work of the Spirit.

Rev. Nicole L. Colvin, M.Div.

Co-Founder/Pastor of Victories of Faith Church
Concord, North Carolina

When I initially signed up to take the Moves of God pageantry course, I had no idea what I was stepping into. After being self-taught with the help of the Holy Spirit in waving praise flags during the COVID shutdown, I knew I needed more education and more guidance. I really didn't know which way to turn after receiving my certification as a Level I Ambassador. So I continued to praise flag, pray for guidance, and worship the Lord wherever the Lord led me. Then out of the blue, while I was on vacation visiting my sister-girlfriend in Delaware, I received a call from Prophetess Kolani, and she said she was led to call me about mentoring me! My spirit started jumping and I bore witness right away. I could tell from the way she spoke that she was being obedient to the Holy Spirit. I recalled from class how discerning Prophetess Kolani was, and I felt like she could always pick up my spirit, no matter how I tried to shield it. There was one class where I knew I was weeping the whole time and I felt her eyes on me, praying for me; so, the connection was already there.

Since I have been under Prophetess Kolani's mentorship, I have learned so much just by observing her and how she carries herself. The research projects she assigns us causes us to really dig deeper under the surface of a thing. When she is ministering, she is so in tune with worship while simultaneously leading others into worship and checking on those she is ministering with. It's been some wonderful moments of worship, and it's caused my own choreography to level up. The last time I ministered, my team and Prophetess Kolani were there, and I felt the wind beneath my wings! The Lord was present and so was my mentor! I believe the Lord was pleased, and I made her proud. She is more than a mentor to me, and I honor, value, and endorse her as my Kingdom sister.

Pastor Charlene Robinson
UNCOMPROMISED LIFE MINISTRY
PROPHETIC EQUIPPING MENTORING STUDENT
SCHOOL OF THE WARRIOR BRIDE

My time being mentored by Prophetess Kolani has been a bountiful gleaning experience. She is empathetic and genuine, and she truly has my spiritual development at heart. Her enthusiasm for the prophetic is contagious. I will be forever grateful for her text messages that held images captioned, "What do you see?" Her gift is to draw the anointing out of a person. She asked me once, "What does God call you?" This quickened me to dig into how I hear the voice of God and better understand how He sees me. (Just *wow*.) This woman of God saw my potential, took me by the hand, listened to my heart, and propelled me in the direction God had for me. I will always be indebted to her for her willingness not just to share the Word by mouth, but to live a life that is a model of God's desires.

I am forever grateful.

Dutiful Servant of God

Denitta Holt

PROPHETIC EQUIPPING MENTORING STUDENT
SCHOOL OF THE WARRIOR BRIDE

A Note from the Author

Hello, Beloved Warrior of God.

It is my pleasure to present to you an opportunity to engage in this book in a way that takes you on a personal supernatural journey. In order to access your true Kingdom identity, you will be activated and challenged to use curiosity, meditation, and prayer. If you are one who journals, you may want to dedicate a journal specifically for this journey. If you tend to write in the margins of your book, we have included some space for you to do that. Whatever your preference is, be purposed to engage in the material, soak up the process, and allow yourself the freedom to be emotionally spontaneous throughout each encounter. Let the Holy Spirit guide you as you access the treasures of heaven stored just for you. Access granted!

Prophetess Kolani

PREFACE

The revelation of Authenticated Kingdom Identity was birthed during the COVID-19 pandemic. During a time when humanity was sheltered in place, siloed, fearful, and desperate for answers, God spoke to me and instructed me to release a message to His children, revealing to them their Kingdom identity. The message He downloaded in me was words of truth, affirmation, comfort, and hope for each individual. I released that message in a teleconference with the theme of "Advancing and Propelling the Kingdom." My lesson was discovering your true Kingdom identity and prophetic purpose in order to advance the Kingdom. The lesson required each individual to dig deep into their identity and unlock knowledge of their prophetic purpose, which is hidden in plain sight. The feedback from the class was a resounding cry of freedom, a renewed confidence to advance, and an earnest desire to continue to dig deeper and learn more about themselves. Correspondingly, God commissioned me to write *Authenticated: Unlocking Your Kingdom Identity and Prophetic Purpose*. This is a book to help others do the work necessary to grow spiritually and advance boldly in their true identity. It is my deepest prayer that all who read this book and engage in the work will become enlightened, equipped, and empowered to live victoriously and fearlessly in your created purpose.

TABLE OF CONTENTS

INTRODUCTION

A name is typically the first gift given to a newborn baby. Traditionally, most of us receive at least two names to identify who we are: our given name (first name) and our surname (last name), the hereditary name common to our specific family. Our names become our primary identifiers, and they play a significant role in shaping not only our self-perception but also our public selves. Our given names are what we are called and taught to answer to, and what essentially differentiate us from other members of our families and social circles.

A given name serves as a declaration over a baby's future, and may also identify natural attributes of the baby evident at birth. In many cultures, babies are named for their physical characteristics, their displayed personality, the circumstances surrounding their birth, or the hope of who they will become. Consider American Deaf culture: when a baby is born, they are given both a sign language name and a traditional hearing name. The sign name serves a dual purpose by providing Deaf people with a way to identify themselves and others in conversation, while also representing "a Deaf person's membership in the Deaf community" (Supalla, 1992, p. 16). Sign names are so strongly connected to the identity of the person that they may change over time as the person's public perception changes. In my conversations with Deaf brothers and sisters. it was very clear that their sign name is not just what they are called, it is who they are and a badge of honor that says, "I belong to the Deaf culture."

We each have a unique spiritual identity, and our name is our banner identifying who we are in the Kingdom of God. When we understand what our whole name means and what we are being called, we will be closer to unlocking our spiritual identity, prophetic purpose, and Kingdom authority. This understanding is essential to developing a healthy self-perception, aligning with God's purpose, and harnessing the power to boldly and strategically advance the Kingdom.

Our surnames are an integral part of our natural identity, and they serve the purpose of identifying our family and history. In order to understand who we are, it's important to understand where we come from. Our family history impacts our self-perception and how we navigate life on earth. If we are deficient in understanding our history, our understanding of our purpose and future will be hindered as well. Identity deficiency is the debilitating injury of the wounded warrior. How can one war for an inheritance without knowing who one is, what one is entitled to, and what one's rank is among the brigade?

Authenticated grants access to an understanding of one's true spiritual identity by decoding the effects of identity crisis in both my own life and the lives of characters in the Bible. As you read this book, you will analyze how identity crisis impacts the whole person spiritually, physically, emotionally, intellectually, socially, and generationally. Each chapter will propel you to reflect, engage, and implement strategies to unlock your unique spiritual identity and prophetic blueprint. This book will challenge you to dig deeper into yourself and your history to discover, analyze, and interpret your spiritual DNA. Every child of God was divinely created to live *in purpose*, empowered with God-appointed gifts and graces inherited from your tribe. You, Beloved, were grafted in to advance the Kingdom of God. It is time to access your spiritual keys, arise, and advance. You have been authenticated. Access granted!

Section One: Called

"Your name will no longer be Jacob," the man told him. "From now on you will be called Israel, because you have fought with God and with men and have won."

-Genesis 32:28, NLT

One: You Have Fought

I was born in a borough of Pittsburgh, where my mother gave me the name Kolani T'Pring Frazier. Initially, I was not given my father's surname, but rather the surname of my maternal grandfather. My childhood memories associated with my name include adults mispronouncing it, kids deriding it, and the retail industry excluding it from personalized merchandise. Consequently, I struggled with identity disconnection, social rejection, and cultural alienation. For many years, I didn't like my name. This negatively shaped my self-perception, causing me to wrestle with low self-esteem. The foundational core of my identity was fractured because I didn't know who I was, and it did not seem to matter what I was called.

I remember the feelings of rejection and insignificance as a young child at amusement parks when I was unable to find my name among the hundreds of keychains on the kiosk. It was also very difficult to embrace African American pride with the constant reminder that mine was not the average "Black" name. I entered my tween years and began to struggle with the stigma of not being "Black enough," which was coupled with accusations of "acting white." To further exacerbate my struggle, some relatives questioned aloud if I was truly family because I didn't have the same last name as my dad. I remember starting to sink into this dark place, but still smiling through it all. I purposed in my heart that I would work hard to make people accept me and make my dad proud of me. This single goal later led to my struggle with perfectionism.

During my formative years through adolescence, many of my issues stemmed simply from not understanding my identity and worth. But God! Thank God the Lord always speaks to His children. The Lord spoke to the child Jeremiah and said, *"Before I formed thee in the belly I knew thee, and before thou camest forth out of the womb I sanctified thee; I have appointed thee a prophet unto the nations"* (Jeremiah 1:5, ASV). It is important to the Lord that the children of God know who they are and how valuable they are. This was true for Jeremiah, and it is also true for you and me. God created and knew me, and he commissioned messengers to tell me, His child, who I was becoming. I remember specific

God-appointed encounters throughout my discovery that gave me both direction and edification.

The first of these encounters was during a World Wrestling Federation (WWF) event I attended when I was around nine years old. I had bought a picture of my favorite female wrestler, the Polynesian Princess, and I was determined to get her autograph. I stood in line for a long time to meet her. When it was my turn, she asked me who she was to write the signature for, so I told her my name. As I began to spell it, she interrupted me excitedly to tell me she knew how to spell it. I was shocked. She then proceeded to tell me that was *her* name too. She said, "That's what 'Polynesian Princess' means; it's Hawaiian and means 'princess of heaven.' That's who we are!"

For the first time in my life, I felt affirmed and special. The "princess" part of the meaning spoke to me as a child more so than "heaven." After all, princesses were in all the best movies. I became proud of my name, embracing it as magical and exotic. Later in life, I would come to realize the meaning of my name was actually bigger than my culture and family.

Although I was armed with the meaning of my name, it didn't resolve the feelings of disconnectedness with my relatives. It was nearly three years after that first God-appointed encounter that my maternal grandmother passed away in front of me. She came home from work, laid on the sofa, closed her eyes to rest, and never awoke. I had been living with her, my grandfather, and two younger cousins. My grandparents had never shown me indifference, and I truly cherish the memory of their love and wisdom. However, I could never shake the feeling that I was not like them. I also battled the spirit of rejection. By the time I turned eleven, I was emotionally broken from familial and social isolation.

During my grandmother's funeral, I decided to go and live with my father. While I was living with my dad, I learned that my mother had been adopted by my grandparents. This actualization highlighted my feelings of being both different and disconnected. I wanted to be a Smith more than ever. I asked my father what his last name meant. He laughed and informed me that it was German for "$#!+." I grappled with that meaning and decided I didn't want to identify with poop. My life was hard enough. For the first time, I felt good that I *didn't* have his last name. I never brought up having my name changed again.

Although I had learned who my relatives were, the experience of living with my father didn't fix the alienation I felt. In many ways, it only exasperated my identity crisis. As a result, I moved back with my mother. However, things were different when I returned. The death of my grandmother had aroused the voice of rejection to speak freely through my grandmother's relatives, who openly ostracized my mother, my brother, and me. I realized that my paternal family was the only link to my identity that I had. I still didn't know who I was, or why I was the way I was.

I was in middle school when my father contacted my mother and requested that my name be changed so that he could add me to his will. My mother agreed to hyphenate my father's surname onto mine, stating that it would be a way to honor both of them. As long as I was acquiring my father's name, I didn't care. My name was changed, and for the first time, I felt a genuine sense of connection to my dad's family and my roots. However, alienation lingered and often manifested its ugly face at paternal family gatherings. I was teased and mocked for my name being hyphenated. I was told I wasn't really a Smith, and I was also taunted and told I wasn't a real Frazier. The rejection took a toll on me mentally, emotionally, and socially.

I entered high school with a whole different attitude and never used my hyphenated name. Years of rejection from relatives, peers, and random adults had shaped my character and choices. I began using rejection as fuel. I learned to let my haters and naysayers provoke me to succeed. It was an unhealthy coping mechanism. Some people build walls; I built a driveshaft. I was driven by power to prove I was the best because I was always passively treated as less than by so many relatives. I was an honor-roll student, acquiring a 4.0 my freshman year. I was determined to prove I belonged. I often made bad choices with friends and boyfriends as a consequence of this need to belong, including becoming sexually active. I was determined to prove my value and to make the naysayers eat their negative words. This toxic thinking and behavior became the drivetrain to my academic success. My junior year, I was positioned in the top 5% of my class.

However, when I was seventeen. the death of my father curtailed my drive. It was September of my senior year of high school. The Greyhound bus ride home seemed longer than usual. At the wake of my father, I remember an elder cousin frankly stating I was not *really* a Smith because my last name was hyphenated. During the viewing of my father's body, I was introduced to siblings much older than me who were readily accepted by relatives as my dad's kids. Yet my aunt looked me in my face and told me, "For the longest time, no one knew who your daddy actually was." It was another layer of rejection. They readily accepted all of these new adult children, whom my father never introduced me to, but they had known me all my life and still rejected me. The effects of rejection lasted many years as I was once again confronted with my identity crisis. I rarely went home after that. I no longer had anything to prove. Consequently, in my senior year, my motivation to succeed academically began to dwindle. My tank began to flash signs of low fuel. Suddenly, I had to dig deep and find an intrinsic, healthy reason to persevere and succeed. It didn't happen overnight. Although I went on to graduate in the top 5% of my class, I continued to struggle with my purpose and identity through my freshman year of college, where I nearly flunked out my second quarter.

I remember one day in class when I saw my last name in a textbook. I am sure I had seen the name Smith hundreds of times before, but this time it was illuminated in a way that made me take notice. It was as if "Smith" were jumping off the page in 3D. I learned that the word "blacksmith" was the origin of the surnames Black and Smith. I also learned that Smith didn't mean what I had been told; rather, it is an English term that means "to smite." To smite means "to strike sharply or heavily especially with the hand or an implement held in the hand" (Merriam-Webster). Bells and whistles and aha bubbles circled my head! That explained so much about my dad's side of the family—the fighting, the strength, their ingenuity to build. I had an epiphany: this is who I am too. A light ignited in me, and a sense of pride enabled me to fully embrace my identity as a Smith. I eventually dropped using the surname Frazier.

For reference's sake, I will mention that Frazier means "of the forest." As a child, I never felt among the trees in my mother's family. Ironically, my grandmother would often say, "Too often, people cannot see the forest for the trees." This idiom speaks to a lack of unity by a group of similar individuals who are close in proximity. I was there as a named member of the tribe, yet we shared neither commonality nor camaraderie. I was close to my immediate four cousins, but that was it. This was the root of my identity crisis; without semblance and fellowship, there is an open door of disunity and opportunity for the enemy to deliver seeds of doubt and confusion. When I learned who I was called to be, I began to heal and close the door of doubt and confusion associated with my identity. This is where I, like Jacob, began to win the strife with men. God was assuring me that heaven called me by name and He was revealing His purpose for me.

Two: You Will Be Called

The identity of each child of God is wrapped up in our unity with heaven. When God created us, it was in His Image (an empty cutout) and His Likeness (semblance) (Exodus 31:12-17, ASV) that He called us out of Himself. Our name identifies and resonates the uniqueness of our created purpose in the spiritual realms. The heavens know each of us by name. Our names declare where we came from and who we are, and they resound the decree of how we will return to God's original intent for us. The creation mandate is rooted in a fundamental Christian belief in destiny to a God-appointed place, where we have not yet arrived. The Jewish faith, in contrast, teaches that destiny is a path back to the original intended place of God's purpose for your life (the past), away from which we have strayed. In the Jewish culture, names are important and very much tied to the journey back to one's destiny. Names serve as a type of symbol for unlocking the blueprints to God's original intent for His Chosen. Even names that may seem to have a negative or unappealing connotation in our culture or our finite understanding serve God's purpose.

Miriam was the elder sister of Moses and Aaron. According to Strong's Hebrew Lexicon (H4813), Miriam is translated as "rebellious" more than seventeen times and "bitter" one time. It would seem that Miriam was labeled and predestined for a life of trouble and tribulation based on what her name means. Why would Jochebed, a new mother, intentionally name her baby girl "rebellious" or "bitter"? Jochebed's name translates from Hebrew as "Jehovah glorified" (Strong's Hebrew Lexicon, H3115). Maybe Jochebed had heard stories of raising kids and the testings of the "terrible twos" to come, or the "trying tweens" of puberty. Alternatively, perhaps the circumstance of slavery provoked a righteous indignation in Jochebed that made her say, "My child will not live the life that I have lived." Regardless, something in Jochebed led her to name her baby girl "rebellious," which may not have been understood by either mom or daughter. But God!

By the time Moses was born, Miriam would have been a school-aged girl. Every time they called for Miriam, they were calling for "rebellion" to come forth. During that time, the king of Egypt set forth a decree ordering the Hebrew midwives to kill all babies born male (Exodus 1:15-19, ASV). Miriam's name can be seen here as a type and shadow of the collective defiance of the midwives. Miriam came to understand the fight with men that her forefather Jacob had endured. She was thrust into a movement of civil disobedience at an age when she should have been playing with dolls and jumping rope.

Imagine being a young girl being forced to participate in the mutiny against the king, watching your mother strive with the authority of man, and having the imminent threat of death lurking around your baby brother. During this women's movement of civil disobedience and rebellion, Miriam was thrust into her prophetic assignment as a midwife to her mother and intercessor for her baby brother Moses. Historically, Miriam became the first woman listed as a prophetess (Exodus 15:22), the only woman mentioned among the lineage of sons in 1 Chronicles 5:28, and the first female leader appointed by God for Israel as recorded in Micah 6.4. Miriam served as a standard against the status quo! Her name and her identity were one and the same, pointing to her prophetic destiny, which would save a nation! Hallelujah.

God's Word illustrates to us that names speak to our predestined prophetic assignment. Similar to Miriam, each one of us must fight the natural order to bring forth the supernatural plan and purpose for our life and for those nations to which we are assigned. Sometimes we may find ourselves wrestling like Jacob with God, or shuffling along blindly led by the Spirit like Saul as we walk to become who we are intended to be. Rest assured, everything in your journey to becoming who you were created to be is either God-ordained or God-allowed. Every trial, tribulation, and test is working for your good. If you stay the course, God will reveal to you His perfect plan for your life.

I remember when God dropped His purpose for me in my belly and told me to start my first ministry assignment. He told me to mentor women in worship and teach them their value as

"Daughters of Divine Design." That single assignment provoked questions of doubt in me. "How can I mentor anyone when I never had a mentor?" "Where do I start?" Those questions lingered unanswered for two years, but women desiring to learn kept coming into my life. Eventually, I enrolled in a biblical training program that provided mentorship and fundamentals of worship through dance. The mentoring was lacking, however, and the only thing I learned from my first assigned mentor was what not to do to those whom God entrusted in my care.

Despite having the worst example of mentorship, that one year of training was a pivotal moment in my life. The curriculum was excellent, and it was during the time of working through those assignments that God revealed Himself as "I Am." He assured me that *He* was my teacher, El Deah, and that no man would be able to take credit for the anointing on my life and who *He* ordained me to be. He also revealed (and continues to reveal) to me who I am in Him, which I refer to as the "You Are factor."

THREE: WHO DO YOU THINK YOU ARE?

One key principle to unlocking the spiritual identity of the "You Are factor" is understanding the spiritual significance of your name. I mentioned previously that I learned that my name is Polynesian and it means "Heaven's Princess." I rolled with that for years, proudly telling people and commanding a sense of dignity because I am the daughter of the King. In 2012, I was in a small prophetic gathering at the Dayton Vineyard Church. One of the women from our intercessory team kept looking at me, then praying, looking at me, and then praying again. After a few minutes of doing that, she asked me the meaning of my name. I proudly sat up straight and told her. She started praying again. She then stated that she kept seeing a vision of me. Here is what she said respectfully:

I see you on a throne with a scepter. The throne is rotating in a circle. On each rotation, you are in a different position. On one rotation you are sitting, and on the next you are standing. The Lord says you go through these two seasons of ruling and resting. Just as your ministry has a duality to it, so does your name. I believe you have only been operating in one facet of your identity. I *challenge* you to do more research on your name. There is more to you and your name than being a princess, and I sense it has more to do with your authority to rule.

I accepted that challenge. I began to comb the internet for my name, modifying the spelling phonetically and culturally to find variations. The traditional Polynesian spelling of my name is Kalani. I discovered that my name is considered a rhythmic name and is used for both genders. It is also a surname for some people. My research led me to learn that Kalani has the following meanings: "The Heavens," "The Queen," The King," and "The Chief."

Another interpretation of Kalani I found was "Commander of the Atmosphere." God revealed to me in that moment that I was the commander of my atmosphere. He told me how I carried my atmosphere into places and changed the atmosphere there. Many of us know "atmosphere" to mean "air," but Merriam-Webster gives these additional synonyms: ambience, halo, aroma, temper, and vibrations. Do you see this? God revealed to me that my presence shifts the mood, smell, attitude, and sound of where I am. This is why El Roi not only protected me, but continues to preserve me from those who would exploit or "pimp" me for their own advancement. My understanding of my name revealed to me why the enemy was determined to destroy my self-perception. In 1979, the enemy tried to physically kill me. When the attempt to assassinate me failed, he sent the demonic forces of hell to keep me entangled in the bondage of identity crisis and emotional turmoil, in order to orchestrate my spiritual death. Beloved, when you know and understand your name and who you are, you take on the spiritual mantle of your prophetic assignment and engage in the battle for your soul.

I was given a third name; in America, we call it a middle name. My middle name, T'Pring, was taken from my mother's favorite television show, *Star Trek*. According to Fandom, T'Pring was the betrothed of the character Spock and the first female Vulcan to appear in the series. T'Pring worked as a treatment specialist, serving people in need at the Vulcan rehabilitation colony. She was characterized as graceful, lithe, and beautiful. Her husband Spock directly characterizes her as "flawlessly logical," which is the highest compliment among Vulcans.

I add this dimension because, despite the fact that T'Pring is a fictional character, I identify with many of her characteristics in my own prophetic identity. Some may argue that you cannot be both prophetic and flawlessly logical. However, God uses me to execute logical plans in the marketplace as an account manager of enterprise businesses, and His wisdom empowers me to execute flawless spiritual warfare strategies in the enemy's camp. Even my middle name, which is based on a fictional character, speaks to a facet of who I was created to be.

Prophet Bobby Conner (2019) challenged the church to know who we are, stating, "We're in a war, but the devil is under our feet if we know who we are. Almighty God and Hateful Hell are asking the Saints of God the same question: 'Who do you think you are?'" The answer to this question is the key to not only why you live, but also how you will live. In this spiritual warfare, you may have found yourself, like Jacob, grappling with the spiritual realm to understand your identity and assignment on earth.

Jacob was at a crossroads in his life. He was leaving the region where God had blessed him and made him wealthy to return to his homeland, which he had fled on bad terms with his twin brother Esau (Genesis 32). Jacob was moving as God told him, but he was also fearful of what his brother would do to him. Jacob was at a crossroads that many of us face, the place where we must decide to move in faith or be paralyzed by fear. In the crossroads, Jacob prayed and reminded the Lord of His Word and His promise to him:

> *Then Jacob prayed, "O God of my grandfather Abraham, and God of my father, Isaac—O LORD, you told me, 'Return to your own land and to your relatives.' And you promised me, 'I will treat you kindly.' I am not worthy of all the unfailing love and faithfulness you have shown to me, your servant. When I left home and crossed the Jordan River, I owned nothing except a walking stick. Now my household fills two large camps! O LORD, please rescue me from the hand of my brother, Esau. I am afraid that he is coming to attack me, along with my wives and children. But you promised me, 'I will surely treat you kindly, and I will multiply your descendants until they become as*

numerous as the sands along the seashore—too many to count.'" (Genesis 32:9-12, NLT)

Jacob's prayer in the crossroads resulted in his encounter with the angel of the Lord. It was in this encounter that Jacob wrestled all night with heaven for a blessing, refusing to let the angel leave without getting what he needed.

> *This left Jacob all alone in the camp, and a man came and wrestled with him until the dawn began to break. When the man saw that he would not win the match, he touched Jacob's hip and wrenched it out of its socket. Then the man said, "Let me go, for the dawn is breaking!" But Jacob said, "I will not let you go unless you bless me." "What is your name?" the man asked. He replied, "Jacob." "Your name will no longer be Jacob," the man told him. "From now on you will be called Israel, because you have fought with God and with men and have won."* (Genesis 32:24-27, NLT)

Jacob wrestled the angel for a blessing, but he was already wealthy. If you don't know who you are, it doesn't matter what you have (Grillo, 2023). Not only do you earn your name, but you also get your breakthrough in the struggle (Willis, 2023). Jacob wrestled in order to get a blessing; as a result, he received the freedom found in the revelation of his true identity.

Our blessing and our identity are intricately woven into a single assignment. This is why knowing our name is so important. The spiritual realm knows who we are, but if we in the physical world, the church, do not know who we are, we will remain ineffective in our assignment to advance the Kingdom of God on earth. It is not enough to pray, "Thy Kingdom come, thy will be done." We must know who we are and the role we play in God's will being done on earth as it is (written) in heaven.

Four: Reflection Activity #1

The first step in advancement is wrestling in the realm between earth and heaven to truly understand who the Lord has called you to be. Before advancing to the next chapter, take some time and pray to God. Sit in your crossroads and remember what God has spoken to you. Recall His Word over your life and speak it aloud back to Him. Take this moment to draw strength and be encouraged to be continually prayerful, both reminding God of His promises and remembering His pardon from sin. His Grace is sufficient. Say a prayer of thanksgiving for your life and created purpose.

Now ask God, "Who am I?" Sit still before the Lord. He may answer right away, or He may lead you to the answer. Now that you have sought Him for your Kingdom identity (faith), seek and research (works) what your name means. Learn your paternal lineage as well as your maternal lineage. Learn the origins of your names and discover any dualities of meaning they may have. Identify the characteristics that those names come with. Pray and journal what the Lord speaks over you and who He calls you. Most importantly, embrace what God leads you to embrace. Remember, on the surface, an interpretation of your name may seem bad, just like one interpretation of Miriam is "rebellious."

Nevertheless, God can use that seemingly "bad" characteristic to advance the Kingdom in a way that may impact a nation. Chuck Pierce (2011) asserts that there is always a redemptive purpose in our name that is revealed when we yield to the Lord and what He wants to do in each one of us.

_____

_____

_____

_____

_____

_____

SECTION TWO: CREATED

"I know what I'm doing. I have it all planned out—plans to take care of you, not abandon you, plans to give you the future you hope for."

-Jeremiah 29:11, MSG

FIVE: IT'S ALL PLANNED OUT

Now that we have learned who we are called, it is important to understand God's plan and purpose for our life. When the Lord formed Adam and Eve, He did so purposefully with a complete blueprint, vision, and mission statement for them. As long as Adam did not eat from the tree of knowledge of good and evil, he had complete access to God's presence and God's blueprint (Genesis 2:17). In architectural jargon, a blueprint is different from a plan. A plan may outline the building and offer basic details, which can be captured in a simple diagram or drawing.

A blueprint, in contrast, is more detailed and scaled. It is often three-dimensional and includes constructional details and the purpose and placement of mechanical details (Wade, 2021). God's blueprint for each one of us is even more detailed and meticulous. He knows us both inside and outside. God's blueprint for Adam and Eve also encompassed a blueprint for you and me. I believe that even today, it is in His divine will to commune with us and give revelation of who we were created to be.

The human experience means that at some point in the journey, everyone goes through identity exploration and discovery, where our soul beckons to understand the "why" of our existence. In the midst of a trial or transition, when life gets tough, or when things aren't going how we envisioned, we question our purpose and existence. Often in these times, the child of God questions God and His plan and provision for our life. We've all been there or will get there eventually.

Despite discouraging circumstances, we must be encouraged and walk by faith. In the throes of life, I have learned to lean into God. I challenge you to do the same. God has assured us in His Word that not only does He see us, but He also predestined everything about us before He released us into this realm. God is so meticulous that He numbered every hair on our head (Matthew 10:30). Even though we are not privy to see God's blueprint, His Word tells us that it has been there from the beginning. We can rest assured that His Word will manifest the blueprint, and no circumstance on earth nor collusion of hell can cause His Word to return to Him void.

When the children of Israel and their king were exiled from Jerusalem and deported to Babylon, it was contrary to what the children of God had envisioned for their lives. They never envisioned that God would allow them to be taken into captivity and remain in it for as long as they did. While they were living under a servitude described as an iron yoke, God had Jeremiah write a letter to the people that didn't really seem like encouragement.

> *"As soon as Babylon's seventy years are up and not a day before, I'll show up and take care of you as I promised and bring you back home. I know what I'm doing. I have it all planned out—plans to take care of you, not abandon you, plans to give you the future you hope for. When you call on me, when you come and pray to me, I'll listen."*
> (Jeremiah 29:10-12, MSG)

This love letter illustrates that suffering is often a prerequisite for salvation. God knows that in our times of suffering, we will seek Him earnestly for answers. God says seventy years would pass before he liberated them. That is seven decades. The biblical significance of the number seventy speaks to establishing an elevated connection, building a community, and sometimes issuing judgment (Killian, 2012). It can be discouraging when we are in our times of suffering, but suffering actually works for our good. In our time of suffering, God says He is readily available to meet with us, listen to us, and provide us with renewed hope. He communes with us and allows the suffering to strengthen us collectively in the process.

No one is exempt from the sharpening iron of suffering, but the Lord reminds us that He is Emmanuel, God with us, and Jehovah Jireh, provider for us. This revelation of God is a key component to shifting our perspective and narrative while we are in suffering. The shift enables us to look at the times of suffering as valleys for testing and equipping. James exhorts us to count seasons of testing as joy because testing of our faith produces patience (James 1:2). It is the patience that enables us to persevere to the mountaintop in victory.

Plans require patience in both devising and executing. God's way doesn't include an all-access pass to the blueprint for our lives. Instead, we walk out each plan in faith and trust. Even Jesus was not privy to the whole blueprint: *"However, no one knows the day or hour when these things will happen, not even the angels in heaven or the Son himself. Only the Father knows"* (Matthew 24:36, NLT). God is on to us. He knows that if He revealed His plans, timeline, and blueprint for each of our lives to us, it wouldn't be any easier for us. In fact, if we are honest with ourselves, if we knew in advance what was required of us to get this anointing, many if not most of us probably would have politely declined. In order to execute God's plan, we must be willing to advance the Kingdom while walking in faith. It is much easier said than done. However, the good news is that God reveals His plan as we trust, walk, and grow in faith.

Every blueprint has a title block that includes its name, creator's name, scale, and date the drawing was created (Taffesse & Kassa, 2005). God's blueprint for your life is your spiritual identity, and it includes four keys: your Creator's name, your name, your date of manifestation on the earth, and your purpose. Your birthday is a key component in God's plan for your life. A birthday is a timestamp of numbers documenting when each of us died from our mother's womb to be born into the world. Consider this: each year has twelve months meticulously segmented by days, hours, minutes, and seconds. Each of those segments are represented by numbers, and each number has a spiritual significance to God for man. Each year has a divine purpose where God unveils part of His blueprint to His children. Each one of us was created in eternity, then strategically placed in time for a specific assignment within God's plan to advance His Kingdom on the earth. Thus, no birthday is by happenstance or accident, but by divine appointment.

Birthdays are God's way to position people for their purpose. Our seasons of testing prepare us along the way to be ready for the greater assignment and the given authority. Although we may become anxious in the waiting and testing phase, it's important for each of us to go through our unique process and allow God to shape us, then reveal us in His appointed time. When we try to usurp this process, we risk hurting others in our immaturity or stunting our own growth by acting prematurely.

SIX: MY HOUR HAS NOT YET COME

When Jesus was twelve years old, he became separated from his parents for three days. Mary and Joseph looked frantically among their family and friends traveling from Jerusalem to Nazareth. They discovered that Jesus had never left Jerusalem, and they found him in the Temple talking among the religious leaders.

His parents didn't know what to think. "Son," his mother said to him, "why have you done this to us? Your father and I have been frantic, searching for you everywhere." "But why did you need to search?" he asked. "Didn't you know that I must be in my Father's house?" But they didn't understand what he meant. Then he returned to Nazareth with them and was obedient to them. And his mother stored all these things in her heart. Jesus grew in wisdom and in stature and in favor with God and all the people. (Luke 2:48-52, NLT)

I love how this story illustrates Jesus's compassion and humility. I am convinced that Jesus saw the anxiety and frustration that He had caused his parents. Jesus perceived that they did not understand or approve of His actions at that moment. It was not the right time. The right thing for Jesus to do was to honor His parents, wait for His time, submit to their authority, and mature in His understanding of being a human placed in time. In this manner, Jesus attained wisdom and favor with both God and man.

In John 2, many years later, Jesus performs His first miracle at a wedding reception. Ironically, Jesus's act is put in motion at the request of His mother Mary. Jesus initially responds to her request, "My hour has not yet come." However, Mother Mary has watched Jesus grow up. She knows His character and potential and believes His time has come. Every child of God has a time when the Lord will release us into ministry. If we continue to walk in the wisdom of those appointed to nurture and teach us, God will give them wisdom, and they will nudge us just at the right moment.

Each of us is challenged to mature in our humanity and attain wisdom in the waiting. We all must go through a journey to arrive at the age of accountability. Discovery of our identity is part of attaining wisdom. Psychologist David Benner (2015) defines identity as not only who we perceive ourselves to be but also who we experience ourselves to be. He further explains that identity is the "I" that each one of us carries within. We began carrying that "I" the moment we were born. The day the Lord released you into time was purposed by His divine design. From the day you were born, you have been acquiring your identity and training to perfect the gifts and graces of your inheritance. Your training from the time you were a child has encompassed various grows and glows marked by times of both suffering and celebration.

Consider the childhood of King David. David was born the youngest of Jesse's eight sons. In 1 Samuel 16, the Lord instructed the prophet Samuel to go to Bethlehem to anoint the next king, whom God had provided for Himself from among the house of Jesse. Samuel blessed Jesse and all of his sons and invited them to a sacrifice. When the time came to anoint the king from among the sons of Jesse, Samuel found that the oil of the anointing would not flow because the Lord had rejected all of the sons before him. Samuel inquired if Jesse had any more sons. It was only after God the Father rejects Jesse's "choice" sons that another son was revealed, David the youngest, who was tending the sheep.

Let's pause right here. Do you see how Jesse had essentially rejected and excluded David from the prophet's blessings? David was not initially invited to come to the ceremony. I am inclined to believe that this was not the first time David was overlooked by his father and made to feel less than his brothers. Jesse's perceptions and God's original intent for David are juxtaposed in this moment. While Jesse sees a little ruddy sheep herder, God sees a warrior king after His own heart. Young David was not considered an option by his family. Familial rejection can derail us from having a healthy self-perception and understanding of our spiritual identity. David's historical context here should affirm in each of us that God can and will use us for His glory and Kingdom advancement.

Regardless of Jesse's rejection of David, God saw and selected David for Himself. In a moment, David went from not being an invited guest to being the chosen Guest of Honor, with all his brothers and fathers bearing witness. The Hebrew word for "chosen" is *raa*. According to Strong's (H7200), one meaning of *raa* is "to be exhibited to." This is the same phrase Abraham used in Genesis 22:8 when explaining to Isaac that God will provide for Himself the lamb. While David was probably accustomed to being overlooked and excluded by his brothers, he continued to grow and thrive under the Lord's grace and mercy. God caused David to be exhibited in spite of being overlooked.

The same is true for you and me. The Lord sees every time in your childhood when you were pressed and crushed from being overlooked, misunderstood, rejected, and even sacrificed by your relatives. God preserved us in the pressing, crafted an oil from the crushing, transformed us in the training, and raised us up as a living sacrifice. He now blesses us and reveals to us that He has chosen us from the beginning. Remember, David was anointed king at a young age, but his hour had not yet come. David had many years of training, triumphs, and trials to complete before he would be transformed and crowned as the king. We are all required to go through a similar process before we are sent out and trusted to do what we were chosen to do.

As a child, I remember always feeling like the odd one out. My suffering included growing up in poverty while being raised by parents who held traditional middle-class values. I was blessed to know all four of my grandparents, who had lived through the Depression and learned to serve the community by creating extended families. I gleaned their values and life lessons at an early age, but I also felt the consequences of their tendency to hoard and amass material things. My grandparents valued being a source for others in need. My parents valued the discipline of working hard and being independent. Growing up, I was the neighborhood kid who had strict rules and a conservative curfew. My mother insisted that I speak proper English and mind my manners. My father habitually lectured me on the importance of land ownership and being financially responsible for myself. Both of my parents were strong in their convictions on higher education being a necessity, not an option. Correspondingly, that meant grooming me for success from a young age. It also came with some pressure to be better than my peers.

I remember being twelve and misunderstood, much like Jesus. I used to try to be a cool kid, but when I used slang or failed to enunciate words at home, I was immediately corrected. Sometimes I was corrected outside, right in front of everyone, which was so embarrassing. This created a cultural conflict for me. Most of my peers spoke slang and used a modified vernacular that was unique to the streets. It was hard to be a child in the hood, but not of the hood. Many peers teased me and said I talked funny, "like white people." On more occasions than I can count, I was accused of trying to be better than others.

The teasing and bullying I endured wasn't exclusive to my peers. I had cousins who teased me for the way I dressed, the way I looked, and the way I talked as well. As a young baby, I became the victim of a family member's vicious dog attack that left my face scarred. It was very hurtful to have my own family members tease me about those scars and joke about bringing the dog around to get me again throughout my adolescent years.

I remember how I cried a lot at the age of twelve, feeling rejected by the world. My father would often tell me I only needed to cry if he whooped me or when he died. He would stick his chest out and bellow, "You don't need their damn approval or their friendship because you aren't like them." I know he was trying to comfort me, and he was proud of me, but his statement caused me to feel more self-conscious. "If I am not like my family, who am I like?" I wondered. I wasn't a talented singer like my mother, who has perfect pitch. I wasn't a willing brawler like my father, who never lost a fight. In the consciousness of who I was, I wasn't like *anyone*. Because I couldn't see myself in those around me, I found strife within myself. Again, I was suffering and face to face with my identity crisis. I battled with a void in my identity from childhood through adolescence, and well into my early twenties. I spent a lot of time collecting pieces of who I wanted to be and trying to mold them into an ideal identity that people would accept and celebrate. Although I struggled, my hour would one day come.

SEVEN: BORN FOR SUCH A TIME

Birthdays are significant milestones in most cultures and are often celebrated with food, family, and friends. My birthday is the seventeenth day of January. Based on my birthday, I learned at an early age that my astrological sign is Capricorn, and people could see in me the many personality traits of my sign. As a child, something in me found it odd that people would try to box me in and expect me to live up to the stereotypes of an astrological goat. I would get a whole new revelation on this many years later.

Growing up, I rarely had a birthday celebration party. Winter birthday parties were nearly nonexistent because I grew up where it was very cold in January, so people wouldn't show up. Alternatively, my mother would throw me a half-birthday party in June. In the very month I was born in 1977, Pittsburgh had the worst and coldest winter on record to date, and the entire east coast suffered one of the worst winter storms in history. I still hear stories from people who were in Miami, Florida, and remember that being the first time they had snow: "Oh, the Blizzard of 1977."

As a child, I often wondered why God would drop me on earth in Pittsburgh during a record-breaking cold wave. I had heard the Bahamas was a very nice warm place, so there were definitely options. Some winters it would be so unbelievably cold on my birthday that I would jokingly ask my mother if I wasn't really adopted from a Bahamian family. She assured me I most certainly was not. For many of my birthdays, it was a day when I turned a year older and celebrated by eating cake with immediate family. My half birthdays were pool parties with family and outdoor grilling. It was so much fun, I always wished June 17 was my real birthday.

I accepted Christ as my Lord and Savior at the age of twenty-four. Early in my walk, I began to study the biblical significance of numbers. I learned that one means unity, seven means completeness and holiness, and seventeen means victory. On June 17, exactly six months after my natural birthday, God gifted me the baptism of the Holy Spirit. My half birthday became my spiritual birthday. It was apparent that God wanted me to understand the significance of the number seventeen in my life. He revealed a key aspect of

His blueprint for my life. In the moment of my baptism, the Holy Spirit spoke through me, first in an unknown tongue, then in an English translation. The English was "Because You First Loved Me." God affirmed me in that moment not only with His love for me, but also with His abiding presence. He let me know He has always been with me from the beginning and He has loved me from the beginning. It was the most comforting feeling I had ever felt. For the first time, I knew I was both loved and significant. I pledged to Him a sold-out life for the rest of my life as a demonstration of my love and gratitude.

Nearly twenty years after my spiritual birthday, I discovered my natural birthday's spiritual significance documented on the Jewish calendar. I was reading a book by Apostle Chuck Pierce, called *A Time to Advance*, where I learned that the Jewish calendar actually outlined covenant encounters between the Creator and His creation. I learned that there are cycles of blessings and appointments, the ordained feasts, fasts, and harvest cycles. This led me to dig deeper into my birth date. I used an online Hebrew calendar to determine what day and time my birth fell on. This knowledge helped me to unlock aspects of my spiritual identity and Kingdom purpose.

Based on my historical research, I was born in the Hebrew month of Tevet on the 27th day. Tevet is the tenth month of the Jewish calendar. Tevet is a wintery season marked by heavy rain and associated with immersion or saturation (Posne, 2018). Many times when I am ministering or in the midst of corporate worship, God will reveal His manifested presence to me in the tangible feeling of being wet or in water, despite the fact that I am actually dry. Other times, He will show me waterfalls and rivers in the Spirit. Where there is no water in the spirit realm, God's presence is absent in the natural realm. In my prayer time, God revealed to me that it would be my responsibility as a prophet to take water into the dry regions. It was fascinating to see in writing that what God had been revealing to me in my prayer closet was a glimpse of His blueprint documented within His holy calendar. I began to understand that our birthdays are appointments of God for man to be revealed for such a time.

"For such a time" is translated from a Hebrew word that means "especially now," having the connotation of certainty and due season (Strong). A birthday is the beginning of the due season and where we pick up our part in the advancement of the Kingdom on earth. The year and day are significant indicators to unlocking our roles and assignments. My study of twenty-seven highlighted the New Testament, which has twenty-seven books. Twenty-seven is the perfect cube of three, or three magnified. Symbolically, the number three means wholeness. I began to understand that God wants me to walk in wholeness and He sanctifies me wholly in my mind, spirit, and body, preserving me for such a time (1 Thessalonians 5:23). The number twenty-seven points to the new wine, the new covenant, and the New Testament, God's blueprint for salvation. God revealed to me how my life is connected in the New Testament plan for salvation.

A spiritual birthday is the day when you and I allowed the doors of our heart to open and our spirits manifested the rebirth. It is the day when we came into supernatural knowledge of our royal inheritance and God began revealing His Kingdom's assignment for us. Even though we live in the dispensation of grace, the blueprint for salvation and redemption is exemplified throughout the Bible. Esther was a young Persian queen, living incognito from her true Jewish identity. One day, she was confronted with a life-or-death situation when she learned about a plot to annihilate her kinsmen and nation. Esther vacillated between the decision to remain incognito or to reveal her true identity and intercede for her people. Intercession would require Esther to disobey the edict and appear before the king uninvited, which was punishable by death. Alternatively, she could stay silent, hidden, do nothing, and witness her entire nation be slaughtered. As she grappled with the consequences of both options, her own cousin Mordecai wrote to her and admonished her to walk in her true identity and have faith in God.

> *"Do not imagine that you in the king's palace can escape any more than all the Jews. For if you remain silent at this time, liberation and rescue will arise for the Jews from another place, and you and your father's house will perish [since you did not help when you had the chance]. And who knows whether you have attained royalty for such a time as this [and for this very purpose]?"* (Esther 4:14-15, AMP)

There comes a time in your Christian journey when you will face a spiritual crossroads. Like Esther, we each get the choice to stay and sit comfortably in the security of our own salvation or to look out beyond ourselves and see a nation that also needs salvation. I love how Mordecai's words, "who knows whether you have attained royalty for such a time as this," serve as a type and shadow to the salvation plan of the New Testament. Salvation brought you and me into the royal priesthood so that we could become secure and comfortable in our Kingdom culture. Additionally, salvation comes with a mandate that we each go and preach the gospel to those who need salvation. Esther's mind was swirling with uncertainty, yet the words of her cousin emphasized the certainty and purpose of her birth and Kingdom assignment. When all was said and done, Esther placed her faith in God, and her decision impacted and saved a nation. God wants us to walk in faith and believe He is going to do a Kingdom work through our lives too.

EIGHT: REFLECTION ACTIVITY #2

PART 1:

The next step in advancement is unlocking the clues to your created position and purpose in time. Before advancing to the next chapter, take some time and pray to God. Sit in your crossroads and remember what God has spoken to you. Recall the hardest decision you've had to make. Reflect on how the Lord brought you through that moment, and how it shaped your testimony. Give thanks. Ask God how He wants to use that experience to get glory out of your life. Ask the Lord to reveal where you need to exercise patience in your process. Forgive yourself for things you see as regret. Ask Him to use your experience to help others. Write down what you hear or describe any pictures that come to mind.

PART 2:

Let's delve into your created timeline. For this activity, you will need information from your birth certificate, a resource on biblical numerology, and access to an online Jewish calendar, like the one found on Chabad.org, or one from the year of your birth. Write down your name. Create a list with the following information:

Name: _____

Your date of birth written in numbers: _____

1. Identify the meaning of the number(s) in your **day** of birth.

    a. The spiritual meaning of the number _____ is:

    _____

    _____

    _____

    b. In the Bible, this points to:

    _____

    _____

    _____

    c. How this resonates with me is:

    _____

    _____

    _____

2. The date I was born aligns with the Jewish month of

    _____ .

    a. What Hebrew letter is associated with this month? How is this letter described?

    _____

_____

_____

b. What are the characteristics found in nature this month? Seasons, weather, etc.

_____

_____

_____

c. What Jewish feasts or holidays are associated with this month?

_____

_____

_____

d. What historical events occur during this month?

_____

_____

_____

e. While learning about this month, I made the following observations about myself:

_____

_____

_____

3. The year I was born is significant in history where I was born because:

_____

_____

_____

a. How did growing up in this time period shape your values,
   beliefs, and habits?

   _____

   _____

   _____

b. What does God want you to keep from the previous list,
   and what does He want you to let go? Breathe.

   _____

   _____

   _____

4. How does what you have learned about the day you were
   created help you understand how God has been speaking to
   you and through you?

   _____

   _____

   _____

   _____

   _____

SECTION THREE: CONNECTED

"This is my covenant with you: I will make you the father of a multitude of nations!"

-Genesis 17:4, NLT

NINE: ABRAHAM'S HEIRS

When I was a child, one of the first songs I learned in church was about Abraham. The song lyrics were simple like a nursery rhyme, and it had basic dance moves to go along with it. I remember the song being fun to sing and entertaining for the adult audience. The lyrics are below:

Father Abraham had many sons
Many sons had Father Abraham

I am one of them, and so are you
So let's just praise the Lord
Right arm

The song would go on to repeat several times with additional body parts added at the end, coupled with a corresponding dance move. By the sixth round, it was complete chaos marked by kids simultaneously marching, singing, bowing, and spinning around in place. The final verse ends with "sit down," which was a relief after being dizzy and hysterical with laughter. I remember as a child always sitting down afterward and asking within myself, "How am I a child of Abraham?" If you haven't noticed by now, I asked a lot of questions as a child. Although the pastor would go on to explain the covenant God made with Abraham, I didn't understand how a covenant umpteen hundred years ago applied to me. Afterall, I was neither Jewish nor a son. The song was fun, but ultimately I dismissed its validity as a reality due to my unanswered questions. I categorized the song like an Aesop fable: something from which we learn moral lessons. I wouldn't discover the truth and personal revelation of this covenant until I was an adult with my own children.

When I joined the church and gave my life to Christ as a young adult, one of the first scriptures I learned was 1 Peter 2:9, *"But you are a chosen generation, a royal priesthood, a holy nation, His own special people, that you may proclaim the praises of Him who called you"* (NKJV). For many years, I focused on the aspect of being *chosen* to be a royal priesthood. The church I was in emphasized living a holy life. These fundamentals were key to my sanctification process and decision making. Nearly twenty years later, I was rereading that same scripture while studying identity and the word "nation" practically jumped off the page. I heard the words "One Nation Under God" and "Father of the Nation." I asked the Holy Spirit, "Why am I only hearing 'nation' and not 'nations'?" That's when the revelation of Abraham's heirs, the holy nation, began to unfold.

In Hebrew, the word for nation is *gôy*. *Gôy* is defined as the non-Hebrew nation and is often translated as "Gentile" (Strong's Hebrew Lexicon, H1471). When God made His covenant with Abraham, it was a decree that the heathen nation would become Abraham's lineage and heirs to his blessing. In simplest form, God sees humanity as two nations, the Hebrews and the non-Hebrews—in other words, those who belong to Him and those who are estranged from Him. This is why Abraham would be the father of many nations; his legacy would encompass people from both nations. In order to understand Abraham's heritage, it's important to understand his lineage. Abraham indeed had many biological sons, eight to be exact. However, only his son Isaac was the heir to God's covenant with Abraham and his wife Sarah, according to Genesis 17:16. Therefore, in order to know the ancestral history of Israel, we follow Isaac's lineage. It is through the patriarchal blessing given to Isaac that we understand the authenticated identity of the Nation of Israel.

Authenticated identity in the Old Testament was established when the patriarchal blessing was spoken by God to Abraham. Isaac, who was the manifested promised son of the blessing, inherited the patriarchal blessing after Abraham's death (Genesis 25:11). We can infer that Abraham spoke a patriarchal blessing over Isaac, reiterating God's covenant and promise. I imagine Abraham fondly telling Isaac the details surrounding his birth and emphasizing the goodness of God. I am positive Isaac heard on many occasions how he was the promised, miracle son. Isaac became the father of twin sons named Esau and Jacob. Later in life, Isaac would in turn speak a patriarchal blessing over Jacob (Genesis 27) and a prophecy over Esau. Jacob fathered twelve sons. From ten of Jacob's sons and his two grandsons, twelve tribes would grow and become the Nation of Israel. Each of the twelve sons received a patriarchal word or blessing from Jacob, which included their identity and a decree over each one's future. The Bible documents the dynasty of the patriarchal blessing from Abraham first, then to Isaac (Genesis 25:11), and concluding with Jacob (Genesis 49). Through Jacob, the great Nation of Israel would endure.

TEN: ABRAHAM'S FOUNDLINGS

God's covenant with Abraham did not stop at the birth of Isaac, but rather it remained a type and shadow of God's blueprint for the new covenant. Today, the Nation of Israel continues to thrive, and God's mission to bring in the foreign nation or non-Hebrews is in full effect. During Pentecost, Jewish law required the first fruits of the harvest in the form of two loaves of leavened bread and a blood offering to be brought to God (Leviticus 23:17). Leaven represents sin, and this offering was unique because leaven was typically forbidden with a blood offering. These loaves were a wave offering, not a burnt offering. The two loaves used at Passover symbolize the two nations, Hebrews and Gentiles, and illustrate the fulfillment of God's covenant with Abraham (Galatians 3:26-28). Through Jesus's death, burial, and resurrection, those lost in the world and dead in sin can be found, called out from their nation, and grafted into The True Vine of New Life.

Remember that you were at that time separated from Christ, alienated from the commonwealth of Israel and strangers to the covenants of promise, having no hope and without God in the world. But now in Christ Jesus you who once were far off have been brought near by the blood of Christ. (Ephesians 2:12-13, ESV)

The Church is the remaining nation of Abraham's inheritance and the Bride of Christ. In this scripture, Paul reminds the church that we are Abraham's foundlings. We were each called out like Abram, away from the ways of our fathers and relatives, and charged to live a holy life. "Holy" means "set apart to the service of God" (Merriam-Webster). The same way God gave Abraham and Sarah a new identity, we inherited a new identity in Christ. Just as God chose Abraham to be the father of the nations, He has chosen each one of us as redemptive heirs, whom He has grafted into Jacob's branch and made recipients of the blessing.

The justification of the Gentile nation required a different approach than the one God used for Israel. Abraham was justified and saved by faith in God and his good works to honor God. In contrast, the Gentile nation is an ethnically mixed bag with no ancestral or historical covenant ties with God. According to Strong (G1482), the Greek word for Gentile is *ethnikos*, which is defined as "the manners or language of foreigners"; those "alien to the worship of the True God." The heathen generation of the Old Testament is the Gentiles spoken of in the New Testament: the nation who does not know God as Sovereign nor as a Father.

Under that circumstance, God sent His Son Jesus as a door to salvation for the Gentile nation.

Through Jesus, all nations are able to receive salvation and are given access to the Kingdom keys. Jesus retains the keys of death and hell in order to control access and offer freedom and everlasting life according to Revelation 1:18-20. The three keys we have access to are knowledge, authority, and power. The key of knowledge gives us access to live a morally excellent, holy life on earth so that we may enter the Kingdom of Heaven in eternity. Jesus references this key in Luke 11:52. The key of authority allows us to bind and loose on earth in order to advance the Kingdom of God (Matthew 16:19). The key of authority works in conjunction with the key of power, also referred to as the Key of David. The one entrusted to possess the key of power is positioned to bear the burden of persecution and judgment.

The prophet Isaiah prophesied that Jesus would have the Key of David put on His shoulder: "Then I will put the key of the house of David on his shoulder; When he opens, no one will shut, When he shuts, no one will open" (Isaiah 22:22 NASB). The authority to manage the House of the Kingdom means one has power, but it also means one has great responsibility to exercise wisdom, judgment, and fairness. Notice that the key of power is placed on the shoulder of Jesus. The shoulders are also the same place that the government would be according to Isaiah 9:6. The shoulder is symbolic of bearing great responsibility or burdens, and the government is a metaphor for rulership. In Isaiah 9:7, it goes on to say that the Key of David is power to exercise justice and fairness. Jesus has given us the keys to walk in knowledge, power, and authority. Carrying the authority of the keys means we accept the burden of them as well. We can rest assured knowing that as we carry the burden, we are never alone. First, we can go directly to the Lord in prayer to get knowledge and revelation. Second, He has sent His Spirit to us, and the Helper empowers us to walk in spiritual authority.

Once the disciples had received the baptism of the Holy Spirit, Jesus commissioned them to walk in their power and serve Him as a witness by testimony (Acts 1:8). He further instructed them to go and exercise their authority over the powers of hell, make disciples, and advance the Kingdom (Luke 10). Notice that the disciples were not commissioned with an identity crisis or lacking knowledge of from whom they came. Each one could trace their lineage back to one of Jacob's sons and identify his tribe. This was imperative because each tribe had gifts, graces, and skills specific to it. God's redemptive plan includes grafting each one of us into our specific tribe. Tribal identity is pivotal to understanding God's blueprint for our life.

It is from our tribe that we access the knowledge of our grace, spiritual gifts, and natural skills. Each tribe has characteristics prophesied to them on pivotal occasions in the Old Testament. The first identifying characteristic is the declaration and name given to each son at birth (Genesis 29, 30, 35). The second identifying moment is Jacob's patriarchal blessing that revealed the character of each son (Genesis 3:28). Additional characteristics are revealed when the prophet Moses blesses the assembly of each tribe in Deuteronomy 33. For our purpose, we will pull facets of each tribe's characterization based on excerpts of the patriarchal blessing found in the Figure 1 below. The meaning of each son's name is also included for reference.

FIGURE 1

JACOB'S SONS	NAME MEANING	JACOB'S PATRIARCHAL BLESSING	RELATED IMAGERY
Reuben	See a son	Unstable and reckless and boiling over like water [you shall not excel or have the preeminence [of the firstborn]	Boiling water; flood
Simeon	The Lord hears	Simeon and Levi are brothers, I will divide and disperse them in Jacob	Bloody swords
Levi	Attached/ Cleave to	See Simeon	See Simeon
Judah	Praise	Judah, you are the one whom your brothers shall praise; Your hand will be on the neck of your enemies; the scepter shall not depart from Judah	Lion; scepter
Dan	A judge	Dan shall judge his people, Dan shall be a serpent in the way, that bites the horse's heels, so that his rider falls backward	Snake; scales of justice
Naphtali	Victorious wrestler	Naphtali is a doe let loose, [a swift warrior]	Deer
Gad	Fortunate	A raiding troop shall raid him, but he shall raid at their heels and assault them [victoriously]	Tents; marauder

JACOB'S SONS	NAME MEANING	JACOB'S PATRIARCHAL BLESSING	RELATED IMAGERY
Asher	Happy	Asher's food [supply] shall be rich and bountiful	Bread; tree
Issachar	There is recompense	When he saw that the resting place was good and that the land was pleasant he bowed his shoulder to bear [burdens], And became a servant at forced labor	Donkey
Zebulun	Exalted	Zebulun shall dwell at the seashore; he shall be a haven for ships	Port; ships
Joseph	Jehovah has added	The archers have bitterly attacked and provoked him; They have shot and harassed him, but his bow remained firm and steady [in the Strength that does not fail], For his arms were made strong…	Well; vine; fruit
Benjamin	Son of Honor	In the morning he devours the prey, And at night he divides the spoil	Wolf
	GENESIS 29; 30; 35:18, AMP	GENESIS 49, AMP	

A close look at the chart reveals how each son was blessed (or not) and commissioned; gifted and skilled; and characterized as a provider, protector, or predator in the father's eyes. It is important to note here that in the book of Exodus, we see that God's redemptive plan brought grace to all the tribes. I believe this is a direct result of the prophet Moses interceding for each tribe. It is under Moses's leadership that we see the tribe of Levi, previously considered a predator, restored as a holy tribe of priests (Exodus 7). Just as the Levites were restored and learned their true identity (to be attached to the Lord), each one of us must also learn our tribe, our true identity, and our God-ordained purpose.

Remember at the beginning of this chapter, I talked about how I questioned how I could be an heir or son of Abraham. In 2019, just before the COVID-19 pandemic, God dropped a sense of urgency in my spirit to read Chuck Pierce's book *A Time to Advance*. It was in my studying of the tribes and months of Pierce's book that God revealed my Kingdom identity, the Lord as the True Vine, and the exact tribe (branch) into which I was grafted. Through the research of my birthday and studying the tribes, God enabled me to see how I was truly a descendant.

My birthday is in January, and based upon the time I was born, I learned that my Hebrew birthday is the 27th day of Tevet. The month of Tevet is associated with the tribe of Dan. Referring back to the chart, we see that Dan's patriarchal blessing stated that he would be a judge and govern. On the Hebrew calendar, the month of Dan is the tenth month. Ten is the number of godly authority (Pierce, 2011). Godly authority can be translated as "godly leadership," as we see in the five-fold gifts found in Ephesians 4. I am an ordained prophet, and my strongest graces include teaching, strategizing and organizing systems, and aligning right-relationships. I am highly sensitive to matters of injustice, inequity, inequality, and inefficiency. In the marketplace, I operate apostolically, creating systems of order and resources for best practices. This is the Dan in me.

As I studied more about the month of Tevet, I learned that the letter of the Hebrew alphabet associated with Tevet is AYIN, which is representative of the eye and spring. Every year during the month of Tevet, Pierce releases the word for letting your good eye see, praying for our leaders, and war with the intention of breaking the power of evil onlookers. For many years, I would issue a prophetic word at the beginning of the year and extract a motto out of that word for my birthday. The purpose was to commit to self-growth and focus in a specific area. One year, it was to not be bothered by things that I cannot control. Another year, it was to set clear boundaries against toxic relationships and behaviors. The year I wrote this book, it was to complete what I had started.

If we revisit the prophecy of Jacob, we see that the tribe of Dan was expected to judge fairly and rule justly. That means Dan must exercise maturity and growth. In studying my tribe, I began to see how my perceived quirks fit into my calling and responsibilities. Remember in chapter one, I shared the prophecy given to me. Part of the prophecy talked about me sitting on a rotating throne. On one rotation I was standing, and the next rotation I was sitting, symbolizing seasons of ruling and resting. To rule means "to determine and declare authoritatively" and "to command or determine judicially" (Merriam-Webster). The word "rest" is a bit deceiving here; it is not to be relaxing or reclining, but rather to be mindfully on watch, gathering intel through observation. This is so true about me. I can be engaged in spiritual warfare and look inactive to the untrained eye. This is how the Lord developed in me the wisdom of a serpent spoken of in Matthew 10:16. Today, I can look back and see how the Lord was revealing my tribe's graces even before I understood what tribe I was in.

In 2018, I had a fire-garment prophetically made. I gave the creator no instructions or visions. On the front of the garment are the words *Lioness Arising*. The creator also commissioned an art piece of a lioness ascending up a mountain on the back. I began to research the lioness and learned some important facts. The lioness is the primary provider for her pride. She has a keen sense for finding food and sensing danger. She is willing to fight when necessary for the sake of her pride. You may say, "But the animal associated with the tribe of Dan is the snake." Good catch!

In Deuteronomy 33, Moses actually calls Dan a lion's whelp, who will leap up from the land of fruitfulness. Some of this language is the same as what Jacob spoke over Judah in Genesis 49:9. Both the lion and the snake have one notable characteristic in common: they are not naturally aggressive toward humans. Both the lion and the snake tend to strike only in fear or protection. That is the same with those in the tribe of Dan. Dan is a rearguard tribe, whose role in warfare is protecting rather than combatting. I bear witness that we are typically cool-headed until we are backed into a corner or identify something as unjust. These things bring out the fight in me, and I will come out striking in order to protect myself or those in need. So while I may not be the willing brawler my father was, I will fight to defend and protect my peace.

ELEVEN: REFLECTION ACTIVITY #3

When you and I were restored, we learned that we were brought into a holy nation. What many of us did not learn is where we were grafted into the family tree. In the previous chapter, we looked at our birthdays, birth month, and the significance of the year we were positioned in time. You learned the name and characteristics of the Hebrew month that corresponds with your birthday on the Gregorian calendar. In order to understand where you were grafted in, we will use that information to determine what your tribe is. Use the chart below to determine which tribe is linked to your Hebrew birth month. Read all of the questions carefully before you begin writing your answer.

FIGURE 2

Month	Hebrew Month	Gregorian Calendar	Tribe
1	Nissan	March/April	Judah
2	Iyar	April/May	Issachar
3	Sivan	May/June	Zebulun
4	Tammuz	June/July	Reuben
5	Av	July/August	Simeon
6	Elul	August/September	Gad
7	Tishrei	September/October	Ephraim
8	Cheshvan	October/November	Manasseh
9	Kislev	November/December	Benjamin
10	Tevet	December/January	Dan
11	Shevat	January/February	Asher
12	Adar	February/March	Naphtali

1. Write down your tribe's name.

   _____

   a. What does the name of the tribe mean (refer to Figure 1)?

      _____

      _____

      _____

   b. Read the patriarchal prophecy spoken over that tribe by Jacob in Genesis 49.

      _____

      _____

      _____

      i. What characteristics do you see in your tribe that you embrace, have overcome, or still struggle with?

         Embrace: _____

         Overcame: _____

         Struggle with: _____

      ii. What personality traits or temperaments do you have that you can connect with that tribe?

         _____

         _____

         _____

iii. Consider the imagery associated with your tribe. How do the characteristics or qualities of the image(s) resonate with who you are and how you behave?

_____

_____

_____

2. What communication characteristics did you discover about yourself that are specific to your tribe? (Keep in mind, your tribe traits may not be the same as a relative in your family. You can be in the same family naturally and spiritually grafted into different tribes.)

_____

_____

_____

a. How do your tribe's communication traits shape how you approach God's people?

_____

_____

_____

b. How does your tribe's communication style impact how you approach the nation that doesn't know God?

_____

_____

_____

3. Deepen your understanding of your month by researching your tribe and month in Hebrew texts and web pages. Use the remaining space to list some of your findings.

_____

_____

_____

_____

_____

SECTION FOUR:
COMMISSIONED

"I am the Vine; you are the branches. The one who remains in Me and I in him bears much fruit, for [otherwise] apart from Me [that is, cut off from vital union with Me] you can do nothing."

-John 15:5, AMP

TWELVE: TAKE YOUR POSITION

Position has always been an important key in God's blueprint for Kingdom growth. From the beginning, the Lord's desire has always been to be close to us. In Genesis 3, we see how the Lord would visit Adam and Eve in the Garden of Eden and talk with them face to face. After the fall of man, sin caused a veil of separation between God's presence and man. As a result, God drove man out of his position in the garden and divorced him from His presence (Genesis 3:24). With few exceptions, including Jacob and Moses, man would not be privy to those intimate encounters with God again until the coming of Jesus.

Jesus's coming reintroduced man to God's value on relationship and communion. Jesus admonished His disciples to remain in Him. Through His sacrifice and resurrection, Jesus became the door that restored man's access to the presence of God. The Hebrew word for both "presence" and "face to face" is *penuel* (Strong's Hebrew Lexicon, H6439). Jesus is the Way and the Bridegroom who reconciled the bride, His Church, back to her rightful position with Him. Although our privileges are restored, Jesus instructs us to wait here as He goes and prepares a place for us (John 14:3). Until He returns for us, we are expected to abide in Him—in other words, remain in position and stay the course no matter what. The word "abide" has a negative connotation: a closer look reveals that the one waiting is bearing a degree of suffering. When one holds one's position, it becomes a matter not only of where one is, but also how one's heart is. Just like the Nation of Israel suffered in Babylon, the redeemed is grafted into the Vine and partakes of the cup of suffering.

In the Old Testament, the position of the heart was a direct reflection of one's faith and values. The children of Israel's heart position through times of suffering and times of blessing determined their progress or stagnation. When I teach about anointing, I use this foundation as a springboard. I tell my students that anointing is crafted in their suffering. The posture and position of your heart in the places of pressing and beating produce either an aroma of praise or an odor of murmuring.

I caution them to conduct themselves, especially through the valleys of life. Conduct is also how one stewards the gifts God has given. Good stewardship manifests the fruit of the Spirit. Mismanagement of the gifts and poor conduct reaps disruption. Consequently, conduct determines if you will abide in or abort your assignment.

Since you are reading this book, I believe you have chosen to abide. Do you know that you are already seated in heavenly places (Ephesians 2:6)? Have you ever wondered how you can be seated in heavenly places, yet still be abiding on earth? The simplest answer is our oneness with Jesus. The more detailed answer is that we are grafted into the position of the twelve tribes that also have designated seats in heaven. Let us remember that at one point in time, each of those twelve tribes was once on earth with responsibilities and roles to fulfill. These roles served both the presence of the Lord and the Nation. Each tribe was assigned a specific position and order by God. Whether they were resting or advancing, each tribe held their assigned position. Figure 3 illustrates an aerial view of how the Nation of Israel's camp was set up according to Numbers 2 and 3. Judah was first and faced the east. You can also see that Levi was at the center of the camp, positioned all around the Tabernacle.

My tribe, Dan, is positioned on the outer north side. When it was time to advance, they were the last tribe to move. They would make sure nothing was left behind, collecting lost things and people in the advance. It is in Dan's DNA to gather the lost, protect the vulnerable, and keep them connected to the whole. I believe that members of this tribe would be our modern-day empaths. Psychologist David Keirsey would probably classify members of the tribe of Dan as the ENFJ (Guardian-Provider) personality type. These are people who essentially feel fulfilled serving others. Keirsey (1998) believed that this personality type is rare in the world, with less than 2%-5% existing on the earth at any time.

FIGURE 3

Encampment of the Tribes

Numbers 2:1-34 & 3:21-38

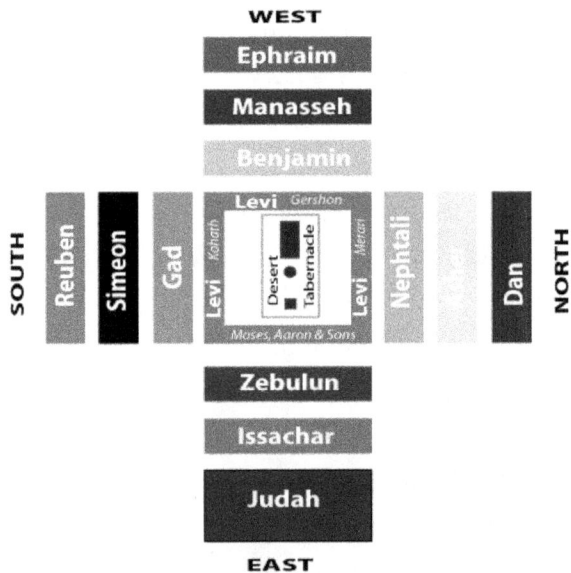

WEST

Ephraim

Manasseh

Benjamin

Levi *Gershon*

Reuben | Simeon | Gad | Levi *Kohath* | Desert | Tabernacle | Levi *Merari* | Nephtali | Dan

Moses, Aaron & Sons

SOUTH   **NORTH**

Zebulun

Issachar

Judah

EAST

In my study of the tribe of Dan, I learned that Dan is not included in Revelation 7. That really confused me. I thought perhaps I had miscalculated or done something wrong. But through research, I learned that this is exclusively a Christian belief, and Jewish beliefs do not hold the exclusion of Dan to the inheritance as a truth. The Holy Spirit led me back to my temperament results and highlighted the small percentage with my personality type. He revealed to me that the rareness of my personality type is part of the redeeming remnant of Dan. As days went on, the Holy Spirit revealed more to me about the tribe of Dan. He stated that because of Dan's close work with Judah in the construction of the Tabernacle, Dan's praise and worship mirrors Judah. It's funny, because based on my own grace and gifts, I initially believed my research would reveal I was from the Tribe of Judah. About a week after that nugget dropped, the Holy Spirit spoke to me about a remnant of Dan found in Africa. I had never heard of that before. However, an internet search led me to a tribe called Dan near the Ivory Coast of West Africa. Genetically, 7% of my DNA breakdown aligns with the region where this modern-day tribe is. I stand in awe today with this discovery.

I am learning more about my true identity day by day. I am also advancing with conviction to keep an open heart toward the People of God based on my information about my tribe's purpose. Through the Holy Spirit's guidance, revelation from my personality test, and the results of my genetic test, I have been bolstered to walk in my purpose and authority. I will never again be made to feel bad when my efforts to bring people together result in people discarding me or rejecting me. Dan is the gatherer of lost things and protector of the vulnerable. I understand that ultimately, I was created to serve, protect, and reestablish what was lost or broken. That is the spiritual DNA of my tribe.

Notice how each tribe is positioned around the Levites, and the presence of the Lord is at the center or heart of the Nation. With God's presence at the center, it didn't matter that they were in the wilderness. They could abide in the suffering and know that God was still providing for them. Read that again. Even though it seems as if they were positioned to protect the Ark and His presence, His abiding presence was actually protecting them. This is what it means to be seated in heavenly places. It means we are confident in the assurance that God's presence is with us in our abiding, so we can position our heart in a posture to release an aroma in our seasons of suffering.

THIRTEEN: PLAY YOUR PART

A commission is a formal written certificate that confers military rank and authority; it grants the holder rights to perform various acts or duties (Merriam-Webster). Once we understand our tribe's position and align ourselves among the proper brigade, we are ready to move in unity when God says go. However, there is that time and space between taking our position and advancing. Remember, God told the children of Israel it would be seventy years before He delivered them from Babylonian captivity. In the meantime, they were expected to play their part.

> *"Build homes, and plan to stay. Plant gardens, and eat the food they produce. Marry and have children. Then find spouses for them so that you may have many grandchildren. Multiply! Do not dwindle away! And work for the peace and prosperity of the city where I sent you into exile. Pray to the Lord for it, for its welfare will determine your welfare."* (Jeremiah 29:5-7, NLT)

God gave them explicit instructions. He said to abide. Build a home and live. When suffering comes, we are not to sit around in despair. God expects us to thrive despite the suffering. He has anointed us for the assignment, which includes the suffering. In the suffering, God expects us to work for peace and pray that the Lord blesses our valley to prosper. This is easier read than done, but it is not impossible.

God has commissioned each of us to play our part. Each tribe had a prescribed skill set that they contributed to the wellbeing of the whole. This enabled the nation to thrive in the valley. Everyone collaborated, which is the same commission Christ commanded the Church to do in Ephesians 4:16. Each of us plays a part. Once you know your tribe's roles, you can better understand the grace upon your life and the gifts you have. Most Christians are familiar with the musical gifts and leadership traits of Judah and the dedication and prophetic worship of Levi. We tend to be less familiar with the other tribes and their specific contributions to the Nation.

In my research of the tribe of Dan, I learned a lot about the people, and I was able to see many facets of my own life woven in the words that I read. The tribe of Dan was positioned in the rear guard. Like all the tribes of Israel, with the exception of the Levites, they were skilled warriors trained in battle. The tribe of Dan protected the Nation from attacks that would come from behind. They were not among the offensive brigade of warriors who executed aggressive lines of attack. They were, in contrast, the defensive warriors who served as lines of protection for the youngest and most vulnerable.

From Exodus 31, I learned the skill set of Dan. Dan was the tribe selected to work with Judah for the construction of the Tabernacle and its furnishings. Dan was a seafaring tribe, and therefore skilled in using fabric, metals, stones, and wood in their work. They were comfortable with negotiations, bartering, and trading. As seafarers, they presumably used stars to navigate and had an excellent sense of direction. The tribe of Dan was made up of blacksmiths who were skilled at metalwork, engraving, weaving, and stonework (Pierce, 2011). I am convinced that while the Children of Israel were in Babylon, the tribe of Dan provided clothing, tools, and furniture as a way to boost the economy and play their part. They may have also negotiated trade deals with the heathen nations. They may not have been faring the sea, but they probably provided many valuable goods necessary for those who were traveling by sea or bartering at the port.

Once I learned this about my tribe, I had an epiphany about why I was so drawn to water. It is in my spiritual DNA to be near water and in the marketplace. I have always loved attending trade shows, shopping in farmer's markets, and finding treasures in flea markets, as well as walking the piers of lakes, rivers, and oceans. I am good at negotiating a bargain. Crafting comes very easy to me. I am by no means a visual artist, but like other members of my tribe, I can repair and upcycle furniture. I am also a self-taught seamstress who can alter sewing patterns to create what I see in the Spirit. I seldom get lost when driving to a place the second time. Not only can I do many creative things, I have an anointing and grace to teach these skills to others. For almost two decades, I trained in the public education system to perfect my skill as a highly qualified teacher. Before I ever entered the profession, God told me it was for my perfecting. My research about my tribe revealed that teaching is also an anointing given to the tribe of Dan.

And the Lord has given both him and Oholiab son of Ahisamach, of the tribe of Dan, the ability to teach their skills to others. The Lord has given them special skills as engravers, designers, embroiderers in blue, purple, and scarlet thread on fine linen cloth, and weavers. (Exodus 35:34-35, NLT)

The tribe of Dan excels as craftsmen, designers, and teachers of their craft. This was so empowering for me! It also made being a Smith a badge of spiritual endearment.

Currently, I work in corporate America solving problems for others and creating accessibility to information and untapped opportunities. In my role, I serve as a customer advocate, a voice within my company, who goes to bat for my clients on the back end of their implementation journey. Essentially, I serve as their rear guard, a layer of protection ensuring their growth and success in the customer journey. As a result of knowing my tribe's part, I am able to see how I am living my commissioned purpose in both the Kingdom and the marketplace. This key of knowledge is so important not only to feel fulfilled in the workplace, but also to know you are moving in rank within your assigned spiritual brigade, doing your part. This is the key to abiding and thriving.

FOURTEEN: REFLECTION ACTIVITY #4

There is a common American expression that says, "When you do what you love, it doesn't feel like work." I believe this to be true. I would go on to add that if you do what you are commissioned by God to do, you will feel fulfilled.

In this next exercise, I am going to challenge you to discover your commission by taking a deep dive into your tribe's brigade. For this exercise, you will need your Bible or an online Bible.

1. Write down the name of your tribe.

    _____

2. Read Moses's blessing over your tribe in Deuteronomy 33.

    a. What blessings have you tapped into that are promised to you?

        _____

        _____

        _____

    b. What blessings do you need to tap into that are promised to you?

        _____

        _____

        _____

    c. If Moses didn't speak a blessing over your tribe, how do you think God is using you as a remnant to carry out the legacy of that tribe?

        _____

        _____

        _____

3. Do a word search in the Bible for your tribe's name to find two significant named people in the Old Testament who belonged to your tribe.

   a. What positions or jobs did each of them hold? How is each described?

   _____

   _____

   _____

   b. What skillset or work-related similarities do you see between these two people and yourself?

   _____

   _____

   _____

4. Consider that we are all commissioned to go. Based on your findings, what vocational calling do you believe your tribe performed?

   a. Are you currently operating in that vocational calling?

   _____

   _____

   _____

   b. Do you feel fulfilled in the position you are doing?

   _____

   _____

   _____

    c. Why or why not?

_____

_____

_____

5. Pray and ask the Holy Spirit to lead you to wisdom and strategy to get into position (marketplace) for your commissioned purpose. Write down the strategy or directions you believe you need to take. Pray over it and steward the Word.

_____

_____

_____

_____

_____

_____

Dig Deeper Bonus Assignment: Take the Keirsey Temperament Sorter Test. At the time this book was written, there were free PDF versions available online. Once you have your results, compare the personality traits with your tribe's characteristics. Jot down your similarities and ahas!

_____

_____

_____

_____

_____

SECTION FIVE: CHOSEN

You didn't choose me, but I've chosen and commissioned
you to go into the world to bear fruit. And your fruit will
last, because whatever you ask of my Father, for my sake,
he will give it to you!

-John 15:16, TPT

FIFTEEN: BE FRUITFUL

When God decided to make man in His image and likeness, the vision was that man would work, be fruitful, multiply, subdue the earth, and have dominion over it (Genesis 1:28). We see Jesus reiterate the mission to the disciples in John 15:16. He affirms that they are the chosen nation sent to bear fruit. Fruit in the Greek is the word *karpos*, defined as that which originates or comes from something, an effect or result. *Karpos* has the connotation of being plucked or chosen (Strong's Greek Lexicon, G2590). Strong goes on further to say that this same word means praises, which are presented to God as a thank offering. Abiding in the Vine means we live a life of praise that is contagious. When we manifest the fruit of the Spirit, according to Galatians 5, we abide and bear fruit. This is the work of the ministry we are chosen to do.

Do you know you were chosen to minister to your family? Your children, parents, spouse, and cantankerous, hard-to-love relatives are all part of your ministry assignment. God has equipped you to live a life before them as a testimony of His saving grace. He has sent you as an example and conduit of His love to be a light in their lives. Your natural family can be the hardest people to win to Christ sometimes, but the soul that is one in your family is the sweetest fruit of all. Now that you are walking in a new understanding of your true identity, you may find it challenging to relate to your natural family. I want to encourage you to keep loving them. I also want to encourage you to lean into your spiritual family for encouragement and equipping.

Kingdom advancement is done by the unity of the brigades as led by the Spirit. Now that you have used the keys to access your identity, it's time to move in your prophetic purpose. You will now need to assess if you are serving the body with your gift according to your tribe. Too often, we simply jump in and serve because there is a need. This portion of the book will serve as a course corrector for those out of position in the church.

Have you ever attended a church that had an unfriendly usher? You know, the one that doesn't smile, doesn't do small talk, and is quick to usher you out if your baby babbles too loud? Maybe you haven't, but I have met many. Perhaps you have met that Sunday school teacher that didn't make things very clear and left you with questions. Perhaps you encountered a pastor or apostle whom no one was allowed to question without being accused of being a Jezebel. I've experienced all of these people in my life. They are the out-of-place ones. I've been there too.

I began to volunteer and express my willingness to serve early in my salvation. I was in my twenties, and it seemed like I was put in the nursery or the young children's ministry every single time. I was good at managing and teaching the youth, but I was absolutely miserable. I felt trapped. It was an exhausting experience every Sunday. At that time, I was also working as a public school teacher. I was so good at teaching that the Christian education leaders wouldn't accept my resignation. Consequently, I left the church to break free from the kids' ministry, so I could just attend church without having to work another day of the week. I left three different churches as a result of this.

After I learned my true identity and purpose, I became stronger at saying no to things in the church that didn't align with my call. I learned that my position as a teacher in the marketplace was not a mandate for me to teach children's ministry in the church. Sometimes we spend a lot of time serving man's vision, and we stray away from the blueprint God has laid out for us. I believe that is what has happened to the unfriendly usher, the aggressive apostle, and the amateur Sunday school teacher: they got stuck serving in a position that wasn't aligned with their prophetic purpose. Before we go on to the next section, take a moment and reflect on the following questions:

- What has God given me the grace to do (e.g., sing, exhort, organize)?

- How am I using my gifts to serve my family in a way that bears fruit?
- How am I using my gifts to serve my spiritual family and advance the Kingdom?
- How am I demonstrating the fruits of the Spirit in the marketplace?

Now ask the Holy Spirit to help you do the things you have just meditated on.

SIXTEEN: ASK

I grew up in poverty. The norms of poverty within a family are pretty simple and universal. Don't ask for anything extra. If you do ask for something, expect the greater likelihood that you are not going to get what you want. I heard "no" a lot growing up. I also lived with "wait" and "Let me think about it." Both were often delayed nos. Consequently, I learned to only ask for things I really needed. Although I did get some things I wanted, it was never in excess. The rules and norms of poverty taught me how to be grateful for things and opportunities I was able to have. I was able to go to camp. I was able to be a Girl Scout for a period of time. We had free community centers where we could play in a safe environment and learn skills. Poverty also taught me that being told no was a normal part of life. This lesson helped me navigate rejection in a healthy way later in life. I learned to work hard for what I need, and to take advantage of opportunities that would help me acquire a better life, such as education, reading, and investing.

As an adult, I still have the core values of working hard and taking advantage of opportunities that help me advance. As a daughter of the King, the one thing I still struggle with as a residue from my poverty background is the word "ask." The Lord once told me in my prayer time that He loves that I am grateful, and He loves me. He then went on to tell me that I never ask Him for anything. It took me a while to realize, after minutes of searching my own finite memory banks, that my prayers don't consist of asking for anything of substance. God has provided me with what I need, so I just don't ask for anything for myself. I didn't realize that was hindering my prosperity. What do I mean? It means I was living life under the mercy of God but not tapping into the blessings and favor of God for my life. Let that soak in. He told me there is a difference in the quality of life. Mercies of God are given every day that we are alive on this side of eternity. The Prophet Jeremiah explained mercies in Lamentations 3:22-23 (KJV):

It is of the LORD's mercies that we are not consumed,
Because his compassions fail not.
They are new every morning: great is thy faithfulness.

Daily God gives His children everything they need. The promises of God for every child of God are His mercies. Some mercies are given outside of salvation because God sees us as His even before we say yes. Think of mercies as provision. It is our responsibility to steward the provision. It is also our privilege to ask Him for things beyond our basic needs. The excess and overflow are the blessings and favor of God. They are given to us so that we may be blessed to bless others and glorify God. There are blessings held up in heaven waiting for us to step into position and voice-activate their release. Once we understand our true identity, we understand that we are the children of a loving Father, who is God of the universe. He has infinite resources that we can tap into for the advancement of the Kingdom on earth and to glorify His name. God's blueprint is so perfect that He installed a failsafe in case we do not know what to ask for: He gave us the Holy Spirit. The Holy Spirit is so much to us, including our Helper, Intercessor, Teacher, and Comforter.

When we don't know what to ask for, the Spirit Himself will pray on our behalf. He will even take a thought or earnest desire back as a prayer request. This recently happened to me. I was thinking within myself, "I would really like to incorporate more fish in my diet. It is one of the things I really miss about being home: the rivers and fresh fish." It was really just me and my private thoughts. The following Saturday, I was walking my dog, and my neighbor called me over to his driveway. When I got there, he asked me if I wanted any fish. He had caught too many and had nowhere to store them. He gave me about eight crappie and two trout, *free.* My neighbor told me he goes up to the lake a lot, and he could start bringing me some fish whenever he goes. I was super excited. I offered to pay him for any he brought back. He answered with a firm, "No, ma'am, you won't. I'll give them to you." As I walked away with my fish, I looked up and said aloud, "Daddy, you are always showing up in unexpected places." His response was, "Ask."

SEVENTEEN: ACCESS GRANTED

"Authenticated" means one has been verified and granted access; it "implies establishing validity by authoritative affirmation or by factual proof" (Merriam-Webster). You are a Kingdom warrior-ambassador, chosen, authenticated, and authorized to advance the Kingdom of God on earth. You have been given the official document from Jesus, the One legally authorized by heaven to send you.

> *Jesus came and told his disciples, "I have been given all authority in heaven and on earth. Therefore, go and make disciples of all the nations, baptizing them in the name of the Father and the Son and the Holy Spirit. Teach these new disciples to obey all the commands I have given you. And be sure of this: I am with you always, even to the end of the age."* (Matthew 28:18-20, NLT)

Jesus has commissioned you, ordained you, and sent you to make disciples. In other words, God said, "Go, Multiply, Abide, and Know!" This is the mandate. This is the passing of the baton. We are now to make earth mirror heaven.

In the beginning of this book, I mentioned that the number seventeen in the Bible means victorious. It is by divine design that this book contains *seventeen* chapters. You are authenticated! You have authority and complete victory over the enemy!

> *"I have told you these things, so that in Me you may have [perfect] peace. In the world you have tribulation and distress and suffering, but be courageous [be confident, be undaunted, be filled with joy]; I have overcome the world." [My conquest is accomplished, My victory abiding.]* (John 16:33, AMP)

The time has come for the Sons and Daughters of God to arise, shine, and slay the head of the enemy. As you take your position and align with the Brigade of Heaven, ask God to heal the land. Creation is awaiting, anticipating, and groaning in expectation for the authentication of God's children (Romans 8). Only the true sons and daughters can free creation from the curse. The time is now. *"Encourage and rebuke with full authority. Let no one disregard or despise you [conduct yourself and your teaching so as to command respect]"* (Titus 2:15, AMP).

It is time to use your keys to access your inheritance. Access has been granted to you. This charge is for me, and this charge is for you:

Ask and keep on asking and it will be given to you; seek and keep on seeking and you will find; knock and keep on knocking and the door will be opened to you. For everyone who keeps on asking receives, and he who keeps on seeking finds, and to him who keeps on knocking, it will be opened. (Matthew 7:7-8, AMP)

Be encouraged and keep your joy in the journey. Remember, He has chosen you. You were built for the assignment and released at the right time. God doesn't make mistakes. He is strategic and intentional. He created you on purpose to war, create, subdue, multiply, and advance from a place of victory. You have been authenticated; it is time to take your place and advance in your prophetic calling and purpose. God says Go!

REFERENCES

REFERENCE SOURCES

Merriam-Webster Dictionary, merriam-webster.com

Strong's Greek Lexicon, blueletterbible.org

Strong's Hebrew Lexicon, blueletterbible.org

OTHER SOURCES

Benner, D. G. (2015). *The gift of being yourself: The sacred call to self-discovery*. Intervarsity Press.

Conner, B. (2019, September 2). *Witchcraft in the church and the presence of God* [Video]. YouTube. https://youtu.be/uzMIJcY2RSI

Fandom. (n.d.). *T'Pring*. Memory Alpha. https://memory-alpha.fandom.com/wiki/T%27Pring

REFERENCES

Keirsey, D. (1998). *Please understand me II: Temperament, character, intelligence.* Prometheus Nemesis.

Killian, G. (2012, July 27). The meaning of seventy - םיעבש. https://www.betemunah.org/seventy.html

Grillo, J. (2023, January 14). *Favor changes the game: Believe for it* [Sermon].

Michal, H. E (1998) Desert encampment of the tribes of Israel. https://www.agapebiblestudy.com/charts/Encampment%20 of%20the%20Twelve%20Tribes%20of%20Israel.htm

Pierce, C. D., Heidler, R. D., & Heidler, L. (2011). *A time to advance: Understanding the significance of the Hebrew tribes and months.* Glory of Zion International, Inc.

Posner, M. (2018). *11 facts about the month of Tevet every Jew should know.* Chabad. https://www.chabad.org/library/article_cdo/ aid/4223896/jewish/11-Facts-About-the-Month-of-Tevet-Every-Jew-Should-Know.htm

Supalla, S. J. (1992). *The book of name signs: Naming in American Sign Language.* Dawnsignpress.

Taffesse, W., & Kassa, L. (2005). *Engineering drawing.* The Carter Center. https://www.cartercenter.org/resources/pdfs/health/ ephti/library/lecture_notes/env_health_science_students/ engineeringdrawing.pdf

Trimm, C. (2008). *The rules of engagement: The art of strategic prayer and spiritual warfare.* Charisma House.

REFERENCES

Wade, O. (2021, October 4). *What's the difference between a plan and a blueprint?* Remodel or Move. https://www.remodelormove. com/whats-the-difference-between-a-plan-and-a-blueprint/

Willis, R. (2023, February 26). *God is calling you back to Bethel* [Sermon].

www.ingramcontent.com/pod-product-compliance
Lightning Source LLC
Chambersburg PA
CBHW071948100426
42736CB00042B/2345